Part memoir, part paean to family, ancestry, and place, Nyquist takes us from home to home, from Sweden to Minnesota to New Mexico, and through time, from before her birth to her parents' death. She asks, how do we ever know the full story of those we love? How are we shaped by geography and family history? With tenderness and grace, she bears witness to her parents' growing frailty, their passing and the emotional aftermath. Like going through a wormhole, Nyquist's poems collapse past and present: a telephone call to her deceased grandmother; meeting her parents by chance on the freeway: "I chose them as a portal to this place." Nyquist describes a spiritual and physical closeness to the dead, better than any heaven. She is our medium, calling forth their voices: "flying back and forth, I'm suspended/Mom visits me in the clouds." Her poems are the umbilical cord between the living and the dead. Red sheets, turquoise, red lipstick, frozen strawberries and those unforgettable roses in the snow, the inextinguishable fire.

--Kendra Tanacea, author of *A Filament Burns in Blue Degrees*

Skeins of memory and images of place haunt this moving tribute to family. Jules provides a narrative of closure, connecting parental life and death with spiritual awareness. The reader shares her vision as the epiphanies flow with rhythm and pace.

--Woody Lewis, author of *Three Lost Souls: Stories about race, class and loneliness* (Gotham Lane, 2016)

Homesick, then is a poetic tribute to the power of place, ancestry, secrets and the ferocious love of family that mark a life lived fully. Jules Nyquist provides a generous feast of language and photography that bears witness to her grandmother's murder 'invisible (until she found me)', the daily details of her parent's long love and aging/deaths (ICU warmed blankets, scooters) and her own soul's journey across the country and through love and rupture, anchored in the color red, pots of cut flowers, piano scores. This is a narrative both specific and universal: the story of a girl who wants to break with convention, a woman who loves nature in a technological age, of dream tortoises who expose lost graves and of underwater conversations with the dead. Memories and secrets are born new, held in the bright light of this book, this offering.

--Tina Carlson, author of *Ground, Wind, This Body*

In *Homesick, Then*, questions such as "Where do you go when you close your eyes?" and "Why do I see it now..." actively engage the reader in this book of poems which is not only concerned with familial absence and presence but the impacts of what is known, what is thought to be known, and the unknowable. From the 1960s to the present, Nyquist explores these and more questions with the courage to look inward while ever looking outward, with sentiment but not sentimentality.

--Claudia M. Stanek, winner of the 2013 Bright Hill Press Chapbook Prize for her manuscript *Language You Refuse to Learn*. http://poeticeffect.com/category/blog/.

Homesick, then

Homesick, then

Jules Nyquist

Beatlick Press

&

Jules' Poetry Playhouse Publications
Albuquerque, NM

Cover photo: Author and her father (John Nyquist), St. Paul, MN 1965
Cover design: Denise Weaver Ross

For my parents
Shirley Ann Nyquist (January 25, 1935 – April 25, 2014)
John Gustave Nyquist, Jr. (July 23, 1929 – October 8, 2014)

For my grandmother
Margaret Adelaide Keppler Lindberg (November 14, 1913 –
      December 26, 1939)
For my grandfather
John Gustave Nyquist, Sr. (March 6, 1875 – July 20, 1953)

Thanks to my cousin Jacie Davis in Georgia for her family stories,
unending support and love. Also to my other cousin Jackie Thompson in
Ft. Madison, Iowa for visiting Margaret's grave with me in 2004 and
adding her notes in addition to Mom's for my family history research.
Thanks to the friends and family who helped me caretake Dad when he
came to Albuquerque in 2014. My brother, Russ Nyquist and sister-in-law
Violet Jackson who drove from Minnesota to Missouri to New Mexico.
Donna Audette and Phil Frisk for hotdish and conversation in Dad's care
center room. Pamela Adams Hirst, Deb Coy, Hal Cupp and Andy Paquet
for cooking and talking with my Dad while I was doing errands. Susan
Paquet for inheriting Dad's walker and naming it "Minnesota John,"
where it has even appeared in a few published stories and poems. My
Crosstown Poets Writing Group, Harmony Home Health & Hospice
nurses and caretakers, and the doctors and staff at Presbyterian Hospital,
Albuquerque. Barbara Byers & Margaret Randall for recommending
Manzano del Sol Good Samaritan Care Center for Dad (Apple of the
Sun). For my rock, then-boyfriend, now husband John Roche.

ISBN-13: 978-1544113531
ISBN-10: 1544113536
Copyright © 2017 Beatlick Press and Jules' Poetry Playhouse Publications

"One knows what one has lost, but not what one may find."

-- George Sand

"How does it feel to be on your own, with no direction home…"

--Bob Dylan

"In China, the lemon is the symbol of death and the lemon table is the place where men gather to talk of death."

--Lynne Segal

"Death can be – dare we say it? – a blessing. The Greeks – who knew everything – knew that immortality without youth was to be feared rather than desired. But who listens to the ancient Greeks? No one. Not even modern Greeks."

--Erica Jong (Fear of Dying)

Table of Contents

Timeline

1901- John Nyquist, Sr. immigrates from Vaxjo, Sweden to East
Chain, MN, U.S. age 18

1929 – John Nyquist, Jr. born in East Chain, MN (author's father)

1935 – Shirley Lindberg Nyquist born in Fort Madison, IA (author's
mother)

1939 – Margaret Lindberg (author's grandmother) dies in Fort
Madison, IA. Shirley (author's mother) is age 4.

1956 – John and Shirley first date in St. Paul, MN

1957 – John and Shirley marry in St. Paul, MN

1959 – first born brother, unnamed, lives 6 hours

1962 – author born in Maplewood, MN (suburb of St. Paul, MN)

1963 – Joan Lindberg (author's aunt, Shirley's sister) dies from
diabetes complications, age 33.

1965 – author's younger brother born in Maplewood, MN

1988 – Milton Lindberg (author's grandfather) dies in Key West, FL

1991 – John Nyquist retires from Taystee Bakery Company and
John and Shirley move to Kimberling City, MO

2011 – author moves to Albuquerque, NM

2014 – April, Shirley (author's mother) dies in Branson, MO

2014 – October, John (author's father) dies in Albuquerque, NM

Locations of interest:
1. St. Paul, MN – author birthplace
2. Fort Madison, IA – mother's birthplace (Shirley Nyquist)
3. East Chain, MN – father's birthplace (John Nyquist, Jr.)
4. Kimberling City, MO – John and Shirley retirement home
5. Albuquerque, NM – author's residence

Author's parents (John and Shirley Nyquist)
Lake Minnetonka, Minneapolis, MN 1956

Orphans

orphans
Swedish conversations
shut out Dad's niece

assimilate with no help from us
they said.
Mom said she was (falsely) adopted.

Blind Date

Dad's friend Frank says his girlfriend
knows Mom from her work as
Secretary to the Commissioner in the
Minnesota Department of Agriculture.

Mom's phone number was "Prospect" something
in St. Paul.
Dad retells the story:
Mom was his "Number One Prospect."

Firstborn Brother

Dad scrapes out the overgrown grass around your grave
with a butter knife
plants marigolds around our last name.

Mom quit her job for your arrival
delivered you into the ground.
I was not the oldest, after all.

We sit on the couch
your baby ink footprints in my lap
our feet unable to touch the floor.

Daughter

She has her father's
bravest sperm.
Go now, into the world of men.

Leave the eyes of your mother
what she saw in him
and be like your Daddy.

735 Bartelmy Lane, Village of Maplewood, St. Paul, MN
author's childhood home, late 1960's

Bartelmy Lane

The white-skinned child sinks into the ground in her own backyard. She is being buried, black dirt rising on top of her. She is under the roses, Dad's roses. Her arm is dangling out, still alive. I see her and reach for her hand, pull her up, the dirt is loose and shakes right off. I go into the house carrying her and we stop to look at all the rooms. There are strangers sitting in the rooms of the house, in the kitchen, living room and bedrooms. I ask, who does this child belong to, is this your child? No, they say, she is not ours. One room has a closed door. I knock. A couple answers from the bedroom. It's the girl's parents. I hand her over, her clothes rumpled but she is smiling. The parents don't even wonder where she was or why she has dirt in her hair. I walk into the backyard of the house and all I want to do is sit and look at the green grass, but there are construction workers there, putting up poles. They say I will be amazed at how quickly a new home goes up, pre-assembled. I say get it out of here, I don't want a new home behind us, this is my parents' home, with the dead elm tree and concrete block patio and tulips planted by the red wood fence in the backyard. My bedroom window faces north, the far-away place before everything burned down, before I could never go back.

Moon Landing

camping at age seven with my parents
in a Minnesota State Park
my younger brother
plays in dirt, we have a campfire

clear night of stars, we can see the moon
bright and white
someone brought a small TV

got an extension cord and plugged it into the men's room outlet
rested it on the picnic table
for all to watch in black and white

a crowd gathers, fellow campers
glimpse the other world of men in space
I look up at the moon to see if anything has changed

On our basement TV at home, the event is re-run a thousand times
I was fascinated that I may be alive
for space travel and moon tourism

My school art project with construction paper,
scissors and glue would take me
anywhere I wanted.

The Other Girls Wear Dresses

She has Barbie dolls too, but mostly they lie naked under her bed or drive imaginary sports cars. Sometimes she papers their shoebox walls with leftover wallpaper or has them sit on inflatable floral pink furniture spread out on the lawn. The other girls, Pamela and Denise, come to visit and her mother wants a photo on the blanket in the grass. Pamela wears a light blue dress, her dark hair flowing, and Denise has her blonde hair tied with a bow. They pose for the camera, sitting politely. She sits with them, squinting into the sun behind her baby blue cat's eye glasses, with the striped slacks her mother made for her cuffed up around her legs, her socks and dark shoes next to the girls' elegant sandals. Little brother is here, time to go, time to play cowboys and Indians.

School

or will clouds
cluster
to cover
her &
the blue wind
gather at her

shoulders she
reads Erica Jong under cloudy
skies, wind
popping clusters
of couples together &
under cover

of trees over
muted windy
professors lecture &
she'll never get clouds
of science bluster
to unwind

her windy
classmates, undercover
crushes fish cluster
in schools girls unlike her
all clouded
with mascara &

lip gloss &
faces to the winding
long road of Beatles cloud
bearing songs to cover
scratched heart, she
clusters

by herself, clustering
couples under &
below trees under her
favorite branches water wind
around her cover
homeroom clouds

endless cluster of names her
body cloudy &
small covering wild wind

Foster Grandma, Neighbor

At ten I sew my own clothes
in the basement.
Pull threads through the eye of the needle
on my mother's machine.

You are the lady across the street
from where Mom grew up,
Payne & Jenks, east side of St. Paul,
a foster mom to Mom when she
desperately needs guidance.

Gathering fabric for the daughters you never had,
the large doll on display
stands in the corner of your living room.

You dressed my mom, Shirley, the blonde,
in blue
her sister, Joan, the brunette,
in pink.

When I am twenty you take me shopping at Sears,
ask me what I like in a sewing machine
and after you buy it,
say it's for me.

I sew my wedding dress four years later.
You are too sick to come to the ceremony
but you see photos of the dress
when I visit you in the hospital.

Mom helps me hem the calf-length skirt
but shortly after, your doll fell over,
divorce ripped my seams,
the thin threads broken.

Box Fan

Where do you go when you close your eyes? Julie wonders. She stares at the big box fan in the window of the diner, the white blades circling so fast that they are one blade, swirling breeze and sunlight into powder that can be swept off the floor. She closes her eyes, facing the fan. The blades penetrate the darkness, spots of white confetti emerge, spinning in circles. She can hear the whoosh of metal blades, the smoothness of the motor, the rattling of the frame. She feels the breeze in her face, her eyelids, her hair is blowing it back. It's supposed to be dark, why does she see whiteness? Her eyes are closed tight, blades turn faster, swirl into specks of light, of paper white confetti in space, spinning in circles. Blue comes in from the corners and swirls around, red comes when she tilts her head and keeps it there, keeps it spinning. Faster it goes, but she can't open her eyes, she has to hit the whiteness. What will it sound like, to pass through the light? The white blades know. They stay silent. *"Open your eyes!"* they whisper, *"open your eyes!"* She doesn't want to, she doesn't want it to stop. She's terrified of the spinning, terrified of the fan, terrified of the rattling frame. She has to hang on for the rush of it, hang on to hit the whiteness. Hit it with all the force she has hidden behind her eyes. At nineteen, what does Julie know about the whiteness, what does she know about making it stop?

A Kind of Courage

What kind of courage is it?
The anxious, scary kind,
the pottery on her aunt's shelf in turquoise blue
chipped on the rim, well-worn and loved
through three generations and now you are responsible
for keeping it safe, handling it to save your life.

What kind of fool takes their life
and leaps into their unfamiliar? It's
a congested kind of dust responsible
for new allergies, a woman who never knew the kinds
of desert plants that would settle into her love
of chamisa, blooming yucca, juniper and incredible blue

sky, blue hovering sadness, blue
disappearing into the Great Lakes. Her life
out of the fog of waiting. How she loved
seeing Dad at the kitchen table, six am, it
was him alone, eating breakfast cereal, kindness
in his hands as she joined him, responsible

for getting up for school, responsible
with Mom and brother still in bed, her blue
eyes join his dream world of working trucks, kinds
of home calling her away even then. Life
someday giving her offices, cubicles, typewriters, it
never stopped with just carbon paper and blue stencils loved

by her Mom's church secretary upper office, love
of the smell of mimeographed bulletins responsible
for news and prayer chains and the next holy season, it
churns them out around the wheel of yellow, blue,
purple, pink and red. She waits for her life
to arrive at the front steps, waits for the boy on the motorcycle, kind

of coming to pick her up, where they kind
of talk and lay down in the green park grass where love
eludes her young body this time. Life
will grow on in years, waiting to be responsible
for her own wedding crystal, her own blue
sky over her grandmother's lost grave in Iowa, it

takes her prairie life and leads her. A kind
of courage, it gives her love of the wind,
her response to chipped blue pottery.

iii.

Shirley Lindberg (Mom) age 1,
and Margaret Keppler Lindberg (Grandma), 1936

"Mrs. Lindberg Taken by Death" is the title of Margaret Keppler Lindberg's obituary in the Fort Madison, Iowa paper, 1936. Author's grandmother.

Calling Grandma
Fort Madison, Iowa, 1939

The old black phone rings
with a long, hollow bell sound – bbbrrrringgggg
She picks up the receiver in its base
substantial in her hand
holds it to her ear and answers.
"Hello?"
She can't hear me.
On my end she's been dead 70 years.
In her time, she hears nothing but static.
Her husband hollers, "who is it?"
"No one. Static." she says.
He doesn't believe her
gets up and grabs the receiver
"Hello?" he asks, "Who is this?"
I listen, as he hears only blackness between us.
He hangs up, severs all communication
before he will take her away from me forever.

High Bridge

The Mississippi shows herself
waiting as a veiled bride
to catch her lover's fall.

Grandpa tried jumping off the St. Paul High Bridge
before I was born.
I never heard the full story, only that
Mom visited him in the hospital.

His ex-wives are scattered in Midwestern cemeteries.
Decades later, he died in his trailer in Key West
his money hidden in the walls.

I Was Born Without Grandmothers

One can scarcely question tears.
Jim Harrison, True North, p. 318

The buildings disappear forever
the church steeples
the train whistle
the swing bridge over
the Mississippi River
in Fort Madison, Iowa

Did she sit here and look at the river
like I am,
eating a cheese sandwich,
reading a book?

Of course she did, my cousin reassures me.
Her footsteps are on these streets
the Lee County Courthouse
her marriage certificate in the thick book
names the witnesses to Margaret and Milton's future.

Three kids, the fourth on the way
cut short –
the police believed you when you said
you fell down the stairs
you were taken by death
Milton fled
married a woman named Grace
moved the family to St. Paul
beat Grace up too, in front of young eyes
luckily she survived, filed for divorce
second stepmother Lillian
with twin daughters
divorced him too

Mom doesn't remember details
was never very close to her dad, she says
understandable, like me, in her own world

26

finds a home with a neighbor
her older brother joins the military
older sister dies of diabetes at age 30
never forgave him

YOU FUCKING BASTARD
will I ever be able to forgive him
like Mom?

In the church
where Margaret attended
I sit in a pew, write in the guest book:
Bless the soul of Margaret A. Keppler Lindberg,
from her granddaughter with love.

This is the church
where Mom was baptized Catholic
and never told
This is the church
where grandma Margaret is buried in the church cemetery
invisible
(until she found me)

The Mississippi submerges the truth
from its beginnings
until it widens to a mile
spits forth secret tears.

Horizons
For my grandmother, Margaret Adelaide Keppler Lindberg

I dreamed you cut your hair. Your neck, white and smooth, says the new life will be easier. The necklace would have been best kept under glass. Turquoise stones circle your neck. The travel brochure mentions silence three times. You ask the devil for a new type of bondage.

The tortoise encounters your hidden grave. Why do I see it now, hidden from view for over sixty years? They pray for you. Carpenters keep hammering. You close your eyes. A man climbs up on the roof. A woman disappears into thin air. You say a spell upon waking. Horizons keep rising every twenty-four hours.

Your exposed skin can be touched only in circles. The tortoise buries herself in the sand. Don't feel pity, name the stones on your neck instead; touch them in the dark. What do I say when I see your empty shell on the beach? I squeeze your hand. They've made you into a bowl, turned you upside down, hung you on the wall.

Lunar Eclipse

The highest goal that humans can achieve is amazement.
Goethe, 1810, Theory of Colors

Tonight Minneapolis transpires into rods and cones
under my pupils.
Wearing a white halo, she offers me steps of gold.
My bicycle takes me to the middle of the Stone Arch Bridge
where I pause.

Purple thoughts tangle in my wind-blown hair and
I realize, for the first time,
that if I jump off this bridge
into the weeping wake,
floating with the river glass,
it will be okay.

Full moon lies bare in the Northeast,
her white light signals my resurrection
She bobs from the fisherman's unseen boat
in a sea of indefinite color
that lacks a word for blue.

The divine is hidden
but on this night
everyone is coming out to watch.

I Sleep on Red Sheets

i.

The soil erodes
your words. You sleep
with the exhumed, the dying.

I am your granddaughter
digging into my memories
for anything good.

You are the woman
in the Fort Madison paper.
I find your obituary on microfiche
sixty years after it appeared
you died of an "illness of unknown duration."

I kneel on your grave.
Which church-goers prayed to St. Joseph
for your blessed soul?

Mom was never told
she was baptized Catholic
and that upset her.

I dream with the taste of fury,
drive five hours
to open the book with the record
of your marriage.
Your names, there,
confirming.

I know you did not fall down the stairs
the day after Christmas
even though your husband said so.

Your baby never came to save the world
        (you lost that too)
You were pregnant when he beat you.

30

Your lips are still bleeding.
I sleep on red sheets.

ii.

Mom was four years old
when you died.
Her older brother stayed silent,
middle sister never forgave him.

Mom's two other step-moms
divorced him.
Grandpa never went to prison.
I spat on his grave in St. Paul.

Mom's niece was beaten by her father
with a two-by-four
hid on the roof
she wouldn't give him the satisfaction
of seeing her cry

Your grave invisible
a few yards away from family plots
until the same day I found you on the map
your cousin noticed your headstone on a visit.

When did I know my walls had turned red?
Daylight hides what happened here last night.

I bury my fingers inside me.
I stand over rivers
calling your name.

iii.

Enraged,
I open my mouth wider.
Stick out my tongue at the bastards.
Buy houseplants, and rugs
to muffle the secrets.

Mom says she forgave her father,
married a kind man.
Grandpa, I never met him.

My uncle never showed up either
a whole slew of cousins
introduced to me at their Mom's funeral.
They never heard your voice.
Another version of Grandpa visited them.

Your story speaks
to ears that don't believe
you died of an illness,
by his hands, the bastard beat you
says you short-changed money

a bad excuse for keeping you silent.
Grandpa ran off,
headed north to St. Paul
a life that failed, hammering nails,
following the money that disappeared.

When meeting my dreams, I try to remember.

In the morning,
I make my own bed.
I sleep on red sheets.

Anna Nyquist (Author's grandmother) at the farmhouse in East Chain, Minnesota. Aprx date 1940's. This house was moved to Fairmont, MN when the farm was sold.

John Nyquist Jr. Elmore Minn. den
26 Feb 1948

Bästa Broder o Svägerska Tack för brevet som
vi fick från eder för -t par veckor sedan, det var
riktigt euru raskande för os ef[ter]som vi ej har
hört något på så lång tid. men [blot] samma
r-- glädjande att höra af eder, att mi befinna
er godt der Hanna i Gamla Sverige, [det] blev
Kan läsa att ja si har varit mycket bättre
till min Hälsa nu för en lång tid, förliaen
-------- var ja [på] Hospitel nästan en månad
hade en svår operation ja hade en clolor för en p--
in sedan o at nade blifvet, m valt så kunna
und--komma fram så de jorde hal på magen
------ ett d-- m-- säte en gummislang igenom
----- hade jo ej kunat lev-t det kostar mycket
at liga på Hospitel så de tog mig hem, så jag var
n 7 veckor måste tiden lag i Bed för ja kunde
gå p-- gå de fick hålla mig om lin-t vi ja inte
kulle falla omkul, sedan tag de mig till bacl--n
en kunnan varje vecka, sedan i September fick
i Sat att gå Tilbaka Till Hospitalet för en annan
p--- så gä var de en månad sedan tog de mig
gå igen sedan fick ja gå dit varannan vecka
en att se ett --ting var som det skule vara
kunde ju vara mycket men att nämma om menni
kan ju se att ja har gått gått igenom mycket lidande

35

Letter written on Dad's High School Stationery (East Chain High School, Fairmont, MN, Class of 1948) from his father, John Nyquist, Sr. to relatives in Sweden. February 26, 1948. Translated from the Swedish. Anna is Dad's mother. Which brother in Sweden is being addressed is unknown.

Dear brother and sister-in-law:

Thanks for the letter which we received from you a few weeks ago. It was a real surprise since we haven't heard anything from you for a long time, at the same time wonderful to hear that all is well with you back in the old country.

I have not been well for some time now, just got back from the hospital where I spent almost a month after having a difficult surgery. I had an accident four years ago and because of that I had a cyst preventing me from going to the bathroom. They had to cut my stomach open to get it out and they put in a tube otherwise I would have died. It is expensive spending time in the hospital so my family brought me home, where I spent most of my time in the tub. Walking I might have fallen unless someone held me around the waist. In September I had to go back for a different reason and stayed a month and now I've been in and out of the hospital every other week. As you can see, I've suffered plenty.

The hospital is far away, 135 English miles (120 Swedish miles), but the road is paved most of the way and we make the journey in less than three hours in the truck. The best part was that my little Anna stayed with me most of the time in the hospital. She is so kind to me for which I am most grateful because there was much work to be done at home. My son, John is so good and interested in working, he will be done with Högskolan (high school) in May when he graduates, examen is called graduation here.

It is very expensive being sick, $1200 but the health is worth more than money.

We've had a cold winter, -20 degrees (F) most of the time, but now it's nice.

Sad to hear that Waldmar aren't feeling well. Have they moved or are they still living in the same place? I hear that Carl has remarried, sad to hear he lost his first wife.

Suppose I could write more, but that will have to wait until next time if we'll live that long. My wife has written a bit about everything else. Nice to hear that your children are so good and busy. I look forward to hearing back from you sometime soon.

Yours truly,

John G. Nyquist (Sr.)

Asparagus

For supper, Dad and I come home with asparagus.
Mom says she never liked it,
thinks it tastes sandy and gritty.
"They don't grow it in sand anymore," Dad says.

On the farm, Dad remembers his mom
yelling at his father every time the horse and plow
stepped over all the seedlings.

Dad says the male shoots come up first
and are pulled,
then only the females are eaten.

It's been over a year since I've seen my parents.
We gather around Mom's table
with steamed asparagus and Hollandaise sauce.
Mom discovers she likes it.

Fowl

Hunting, Dad brought home pheasants
I'd stroke their colorful feathers
on the patio
while our golden lab, Blondie
proudly wagged her tail.

A Minnesota autumn saw pheasants hiding in cornfields
Dad and Frank and the other men walked
through the dried stalks
the dogs flushing them out.

I was young, in my single digits of age
and remember grouse brought home too
but ring-necked peasants were the superior bird
for the dinner plate
my kid-appetite never liked.

As an adult I call Dad to ask him about pheasants
I am living in Albuquerque
and here pheasants are exotic,
quail are common.
I see them running in groups of four or five
when we go ballooning.

Dad tells me the story of his family plowing
down the cornstalks before each winter
when he was on the farm.
Corn bores would destroy the crop
seeking the sugar.
No more habitat left for farmer or hunter.

v.

View from parent's deck – Table Rock Lake
Kimberling City, Missouri

Summertime in the Ozarks

Hot and humid
Katydids sing in the trees
Frogs croak in the pond
Home grown peaches ripe on the trees
Ice cream while sitting on the porch
Summer in the Ozarks.

Poem written by Dad
John Gustave Nyquist, Jr.
July 17, 2013 – Kimberling City, Missouri

Freeway

What are the chances
of meeting my parents on the freeway?
Our cars side by side,

their out-of-state plates move
ahead of me,
roll on across

farmer's soil, almost to Iowa.
What are the chances I chose them
as my portal to this place

two orphans, set up on a blind date?
Hay bales, cornfields, barns –
we have the road to ourselves.

**Watching the Sunset with Dad on the Deck
in the Ozarks Overlooking Table Rock Lake**

We talk of crows.
Their cackling gossip
scatters across the oak trees.

Tiny lizards crawl out of cracks
between the boards to warm themselves
in the sun. I try to catch one

and you say, "throw a towel over him."
Blue hills up and down the hollow,
wear mown strips of cut trees. Power lines

tattoo the hilltops. The locals call the
scalped hills *baldknobbers*
and turkey vultures glide low on the rising air.

I count five, six, then seven of them.
They swoop in, and I squirm in my chair.
You say they smell natural gas line leaks.

They float in spirals, signals for the energy company.
The stealth bomber base is just miles away
and the 5 &10 sells Confederate flags.

Tar paper shacks dot the backroads
and Jesus runs for office. His name is on
lawn signs all over the place.

We sit side by side, father and daughter.
Here is where you retire,
far enough away to have out of state plates.

What is it?

What kind of balance is it
that shatters like glass
flows like a river of red
bloody or joyful?
Her mood of the day
(daring or shy) depends

on nothing. A hawk depends
on wind to glide it
doesn't worry day to day
about what is broken glass
anxious about a full
cup or a half, red

or blue. She mostly feels red
disappears into edges that depend
on others not seeing her full
of flowers in a blue vase. It
helps to wear dark glasses
when outside during the day.

What kind of day
is it when she sees in red
and breaks her glasses
blurry vision, it all depends
on devices to aid her, help it
all along as she ages. Thankful

for friends, living parents, a full
heart of a man loving her day
by day the balance swings, it
turns solid, then liquid, then red
gas, blood, flowing or not, depends
if she's in menopause or not, glass

ceiling in career, breaking glass
gives her strength, she can joyfully
do whatever she wants. Deepens
with every year. The days
have no names, no numbers, they only redden
as a rash overtakes her. It's

time to depend on a smooth glass table
cover it with fabric, full of
dishes by day, read books at night.

Roses

Dad picks roses
for Mom from
the garden to put
in a vase on her table
but by end of April the snow
swept up the cornstalks

the latest anyone with corn
had seen snow, the roses
covered the doorstep the snow
didn't get to and from
Dad's parent's kitchen table
he looked out at his dad putting

the stalks upright, he put
the yellowed leaves of stalks
that would come back, tabled
around after the sun rose
again blooming, going from
spring and planting to snow

within a week of snow
it melted and the corn was off, put
back on track from
seasons into growing corn
knee-high by July 4th, rising
up for glory, tables

of produce, sweet corn tabled
under melting snow
but we can't eat roses
we can only put
them out as a memorial to lost corn,
lost names, lost graves from

one city to the next, from
moving the family farmhouse table
moving the whole house surrounded by corn-
fields where little boys grow up to shovel snow
and fix semi-trucks, work construction, put
food on the table with a vase of roses

in the middle for Mom, covered from snow
her table set for guests that never came, put
out the corn, the butter, the salt, the roses.

Sunday Paper

Mom fell and broke her hip
slipped on wet grass on the front lawn
while getting the Sunday paper

neighbor called 911
hip surgery, rehab, infections, ICU

I call her,
rush on a plane, wake her up
but she dies

Dad cancels the paper subscription
buys a tablet on-line from Wal-Mart
learns to touch the screen
read the paper
but we can't touch her anymore.

Flesh

When the doctor lifts up the sheet and I see your bare leg
surprisingly tan and youthful looking
I wonder when I last saw any of your flesh
besides your face and hands.

A mother-daughter thing I missed,
going shopping, we never did that much we lived apart
and when I did take you to the department store
to look for clothes, I craved that intimacy.

Intimacy that was lost when you bought my clothes
for school and I begged for styles I couldn't have
and learned to sew my own and you taught me
how to sew and embroider my jeans

showed me how to shave with a pink electric
razor from Sears in the family bathroom
tucked away in its case under the sink
so Dad and brother wouldn't know.

All of us in pajamas and robes on a Sunday morning
reading the paper, rushing off to church,
we had to get dressed for the public place
to show our spirit, sometimes Dad stayed home.

I helped you up the stairs to my guest room
for your overnight visits, anticipation hundreds of miles
in the making and you're in your underwear
and robe asking me to rub your shoulders

and you are so tiny, when did you shrink
and become so fragile, when do we lose our bodies
to others who poke and prod and ask before they examine us
with some sort of test to see if our flesh is behaving

when did your hands start to shake
your perfect penmanship, your familiar handwriting
your lists of things to do that will never get done
the magazine left unread, you had to go

somewhere where there is no flesh
no privacy, you let us all go and you didn't get to say
what you wanted, it all happened so fast
we were left standing with your flesh.

Eating Again

The dying don't want our food.
They push away the trays
suck on ice
refuse to touch ice cream.

After the hospital visit
Dad and I go out to eat.
He didn't want much.
I had a craving for steak.

I rubbed Mom's feet in her yellow hospital-issued socks
covered her with warm blankets in the ICU
held her hand, kissed her forehead
her gray curls so delicate
and I leave on the plane the next morning because
I have to take care of myself
for just a weekend
and hope she'll be there when I come back.

My boyfriend calls and says I'll feel better
when I can talk to her again on the phone
That is unimaginable to me right now
and that's when I know
she won't make it.
She's not going to eat again.

Hearing

It was Wednesday
I helped you put in your hearing aids, adjust the wires
in the hospital bed
your hair so soft and light, I said
I'd see you in the morning
walked out with Dad.

How was I to know it would be the last time?
The morning of my flight they said not to come
you were too sick.
How could I say anything to Dad?
He's on the phone calling me at my layover in O'Hare,
I tell him it will be alright.

How would I know
you'd die on Friday?
I wouldn't be there on the other end
of your caption-phone that had subtitles
translating my words
recording our conversations to scroll through later.
Hearing is the last of the senses to go.
What did you hear?

I dream of you airborne
on my flight of dark skies
when Dad came to live with me.
He brought your hearing aids in a box
thinking he'd use them someday.

Today I gave them to my audiologist
to pass on to someone in hospice, or for parts.
I've inherited your hearing loss.
My new demo aids pick up calls on my iphone,
I connect with others still here.

What would you say, Mom, about this new technology?
How far will the sound waves have to travel
for you to hear me?

On the Morning of Mom's Memorial Service, We Make Love

My body is wrapped around yours on the guest room bed
Dad sleeps in the other room
I wonder how he feels without her
half a parenthesis
missing
unsaid.

Lipstick

I stole mom's red lipstick
from her bureau drawer,
took it after her death.

Dad says clean out her stuff
from the bathroom
so I do, wonder why
I would keep her makeup
toss it all except for this tube
of drug store brand red
twist it up from the case
hear her voice whisper
from the mirror.

My lips are not her lips
my lips ask why and she answers.
Our lips want attention, we are both cynical.
She yelled at me for being sassy,
she sings out her pain and I listen.

Her lips are bright red like the tomatoes
she loved but couldn't eat, too acidic.
She washed my mouth out with soap
because of a swear word.

I try to remember the goodnight kisses
tucking me into bed,
her last kiss from Dad on the lips
in the hospital room, I'm a witness.

This shade isn't my color
but I take the lipstick anyway
to wear on some special occasion
that requires red.

Widow

Dad asks me
to take down the photo of him and Mom
and put one of just him
on their Facebook page.
I am surprised this is happening so soon

Neighbor and church ladies
at Mom's funeral
hover

57 years of marriage
pulled out from under him.

Vow to Poetry

Inspired by Anne Waldman's "Marriage: a Sentence (Stereo)"

Marriage, marriage is taking a vow, vow, my voice, voice married to poetry, poetry, call, call, ring, ring, it keeps calling me, poetry. When I was single and free and drifting, pulling out of that snowbank city with all my belongings in my car packed, packed, driving, driving, driving to freedom, freedom, open, open road, wild desert lifelong dream. Dream of where to spend the night and then ARRIVE. Keys to apartment, lease, moving van, my stuff, stuff, filling up. Too loud, too, too loud upstairs, the neighbors and why not look around for a house and then a man shows up and why not date and fly across the country, why not? I could have kept on driving but took a vow, vow, to keep going, going with the man, bought my house and now it's marriage to the house and it filled, filled, filled up with books, books, books and an old stereo that used to be on the floor and now I don't sit on the floor anymore. I write, write in early, early morning before work and watch the sunrise and wonder how I can survive if I quit and keep all the stuff and the house and the man and will we both drive out of town in the sunset but where would we go? We would go to poetry, the place of poetry, our vows to poetry.

Should have visited dear old Dad for his July birthday, road trip, trip, tripping but instead had a book launch and felt guilty, guilty, and then Dad sent flowers for my book and it was so sweet, sweet and he never did anything like that before from him and Mom and now I sleep, sleep and write them letters: Dear Dad: Dear Mom: Dear Mom and Dad: I miss you, sorry I can't make the trip, life got too busy, I don't have enough vacation time, but I called you instead, I made a vow, vow, vow to keep calling you every week, then every day for awhile, before when I used to drive across state lines by myself, my once a year commitment, then it was maybe more, then emails replaced the paper and Mom sent all the emails and I never emailed Dad but he told stories on the phone and nothing got put in books or photo albums anymore, it's all in the ether, ether of space, space, breaths off into space, bouncing off the walls, your voices echo into space.

57

vi.

Dad on scooter, Albuquerque, 2014

Slumber Party

Think of it as a giant slumber party
      Dad comes to my house
            my brother drives 850 miles in a day
we'll plan it all out, it will be fun

Weekend before arrival
I read poems in Las Vegas, NM
with Gary, Amalio, Tony

           Dad can't find his cell
           phone
           the dentures missing
           keep looking, I say
           over the phone

Writing group helps me
research caregivers

           Dad says
             "I'm in shock"

I call to find doctors for him
transfer medical records

I'd rather read about nuclear war
write those kind of poems
than deal with dad's doctors

           Work says I can use
           FMLA up to 12
           weeks unpaid leave
           yeah right so all it
           really means is

Traveling friends stay overnight
They are easy guests
We go out for beers.

           I won't lose my job.
           I still have to put in
           time to pay bills.

How many errands can
I get caught up on before he arrives?

           Dad says to
           order a hospital bed
           for my living room
           use his credit card
           will Medicare pay?

My last night alone

           brother packs Dad's
           things
           in plastic tubs, try to
           fit it all

                    in the car

I make soup

work, wait   Dad calls from the
                            road
                            they don't get going
                            till 9:30 am

                            Dad calls me every
                            hour
                            keep driving

11 pm they arrive
                Dad crawls out from a pile of pillows, he's so weak
                What have we done?
                          Oxygen machine, scooter, phone, half his
                          dentures
                          Pacemaker monitor, land line, walker, cane
                          Dad eats soup at 5,000 feet

The Happy Wanderer

I drive Dad in my car
so he can roll down the window
feel the sun on his arm
the wind in his hair
the expanse of the desert
a new city for him to call home --
        Albuquerque.

Cruise down Fourth Street, the old Route 66
with the radio on
his eyes sparkle when he wears
his Route 66 cap.

Dad's arm would turn brown
the one that rested on the open window
driving us across the country
on our many road trips
in the station wagon
His favorite song, The Happy Wanderer

The Old Country

You talk in Swedish lying in your hospital bed in my living room
I didn't know you knew so much
you didn't admit

Now the nightmares bring you back to your youth
You are helping your father on the farm
the stories of hypnotizing chickens are true

I try to get you to take the anti-anxiety meds
but you don't want them, you don't want to get up
you wake me in the dark
buzzing my intercom upstairs
thinking the house is on fire and they are out to get us

You spit out your food like a baby
and I must be your mother,
how do I get you to sign documents, things undone
you want a clock on the wall so you will know
what year you were born
when the recliner chair arrives on line you never sit in it
you are too weak, it sits in the corner
nebulizer by your bed
where are you sleeping?

You ask me how long this will last
I bring my friends in to see you, to talk, to watch you
so I can pick up your prescriptions
I can't leave you alone anymore

You are back on the farm
with your brother, your sisters, you are the youngest
You want a dog, like the one you had as a kid
the spotted one, our family dalmation
yes, you can have your own house near me
you never got to visit the old country.

Pause

Me – NO – pause – pause
Dad is a naked stranger standing
in my living room
home care nurse Brian
bathing him.

Insiders, we rarely leave the house.
When I go outside, as an older woman, I turn invisible.

Dad is desperate, gasping
for air
for my voice,
rings the intercom
in the middle of the night

No, Dad, it's only a dream
I'm your daughter
hallucinations
me – NO – pause – pause

migraine needles in my head
fire flashes burning
bleeding, the doc says yes
the lab results came back
I'm officially in menopause
pause – pause – spinning

Nourishment

Mechanical softness
is processed into round blobs
on your hospital plate.
Piled up like mashed potatoes, but orange
or brown or green.

A waffle, golden and pressed into a grid.
Does it have syrup inside?
It tastes like waffle, but eyes deceive.
Dad, you ask me to bring you a cake to celebrate
your last night in this place.

Strong enough for rehab, a future
of new dentures, grilled steak.
No more industrial creamed corn, jello or pudding.
A slot machine feeding of pills
with unseen warnings.

"Nourishment" is the actual sign
on the break room wall down the hall.
The refrigerator is filled with Ensure and apple juice
labeled "For Patients Only."
I discover it is here I can get my hot water and tea.

My smoothie from home helps you endure tonight.
Tomorrow I will stop by the bakery
to bring you a perfect, frosted slice of carrot cake.

POA

You have three minutes to decide
what to do with your Dad's life.
Didn't they tell you?

Read up on cardiopulmonary heart failure,
anxiety, broken heart
it's 5 am he's non-responsive in bed

Do you want the nurse to call the hospital?
What does he want, did he tell you?
They want to know.

Hey doc, why is Mom in ICU
Why did you mess up her meds
She's diabetic, did they tell you

What's the latest infection?
Only the bladder, then wait to watch, monitor
test her kidneys, hook her up to every conceivable

machine, she says her hip is in pain
someone please explain what is going on
call the nurse again, how could she be so sick?

Dad tries to explain what the doc said
call the nurse again try to get a straight answer
at the airport, no quiet place to talk

watch the baggage handler at O'Hare
Dad calls sobbing, he's losing his partner
she's Mom, he's never called Mom his 'partner' before

What is septic shock?
Now you know, you looked it up on-line
mayoclinic.com, 24/7 nurse line

the doc wants to know what you want to do
what did he sign
Dad says to let her go, take out the respirator

they put in her after I left
Mom was supposed to come home today
now she's going home to the other place

flying back and forth, I'm suspended
Mom visits me in the clouds
Youthful and floating like a fairy

Don't worry, I tell her, I'll water your plants
take care of Dad
bring him to live with me.

Don't call the hospital, I tell the nurse
I'm on my way, driving now to see Dad
he never wanted to be stuck

in a nursing home, we did talk about that
he signed the POA
I'm on my way

Dad, can you hear me?
I hold your hand, you're willing yourself away
to join Mom, going home.

"You can go to work now," you say
"I'll be fine, honey."
No, Dad, you can't, you have to sign this check

You have visitors coming
tomorrow or making plans to get here
they are too late

you turn to ashes
sitting on the hall table
in the flowery jar.

No Photos Allowed

I.

Dad's camera was poised around his neck
ready for a new adventure on the Rail Runner
visiting me in Albuquerque with Mom, a quick trip
to Santa Fe, ice cream, too much walking.

Ride the rails back to another photo of my house
proud daughter to have you as guests
you sleep in comfort on the new mattress
I bought just for you.

II.

Paramedics
wheel you out on a stretcher
your camera left behind, a few photos left
on your digital screen: sunflowers I sent you
to escape the bright yellow loneliness
after Mom died.
The conductor calls, no photos allowed.
Your last road trip
no suitcase, no clothes, no body.
Will you remember the family station wagon
leaving early morning
us kids in sleeping bags with the dog?
We wake up in South Dakota.

What colors await you where you are going
are they captured in your new memory card?
A journey with no beginning or end
never to be developed or sent
to the other side to share.
No worry about a mattress
Your camera is left behind.

Celestial

This morning, your voice was clear on your cell.
I could finally understand you.

Over lunch, I feed you.
You don't want to leave your bed.
Yesterday,
I wheeled you out in the garden over lunch.
Manzano del Sol Village has blooming roses in the courtyard.
Roses are your favorites, what you would bring to Mom.
This is the best gift I could give you, you said, as I brought you
        outside.
I am your little apple,
        manzano, of your eye.

I work in the conference room,
get to know the staff.
You worry about how long Medicare will pay for your room
Don't worry, I say, I want you out of here soon.

One day at dinner, you are not responding.
I hold your familiar hand, I know you hear me.
You make faces, scrunching.
Shirley, my Mom, is calling.
You have to go find her.

More voices on the phone from those on this planet.
They will drive or fly to be here soon. You're not listening.
When we were kids, you packed up the car to leave on the family
vacation,
        it was always on your own terms.
You are still stubborn. When you and Mom came to visit me
I remember the morning you woke me and my boyfriend up in bed
refused breakfast
said you had to be on the road
just left us,
standing in pajamas.
I cried.

Remember last week when we saw the two tortoises on the
courtyard lawn?
They are totems of deep meditation to another land.

Clouds over full moon.
Lunar Eclipse.
　　　　　I drive home.　　Feel a premonition.

The next morning at 5:05 am the nurse calls.
None of us made it in time to be with you.
This time, the sky felt truly empty.

Watch

on your deathbed
Dad I collect your watch
from the bedside table
only a few hours before
it was on your left wrist
I was holding your hand
a couple weeks before that
I went to the mall to get
a new battery you asked for
so your watch would last
another year
keep perfect time
now I know forever
you died at 5:05 am
did the nurse check
your watch or hers
by your bedside
while I was asleep
I'll never know
your watch now rests
in your black bag
of trinkets in my closet
I stroke your watch
like I once stroked your hand.

At the Funeral Home

"Your father's mother's name?"
I'm asked by the funeral director
I pause. I should know my family history
ones I never met
My grandmother died after Dad was in high school,
no wonder he was lonely
lived with niece's parents for awhile
building a boat in the basement
to carry him down the river in Fairmont, Minnesota
born at home, died here in my dreams in the desert
New Mexico immortalized on Dad's death certificate.

Mom kept good records, the family data sheet I carry in my purse
for occasions such as this when my mind goes blank
she had it all written down for when I need it.
Except she forgot that her attorney died many years ago.

I was with Dad for Mom's paperwork
now I'm alone with Dad's, have to get it right.

"Your father's mother's name?"
the funeral director is waiting for my answer.
"Anna Lantz," I reply.

Bedside

At the bedside memorial service
Dad isn't really there
But Mom would have liked it
The chaplain reads the generic Lord's Prayer
So even though we walk through the valley
Of the shadow of death
We will comfort each other
Strangers
Nurses
The funeral home guy anxiously waiting
To wheel out Dad's body
Called only an hour before with help from the
Chaplain on staff on where to find the phone numbers
To begin such a long journey
I pack Dad's one suitcase of clothes
Donna was stuck in traffic
We go out to breakfast
I make endless phone calls
Until I can't sleep
It is truly lonely
Dad was always somewhere
Even if he wasn't with me

Kimberling City, Missouri

We enter my parent's house
Using the garage door code.
Dad's car is parked inside, battery dead
It is eerie being here without them.

I call my brother, who is driving and will arrive tomorrow,
as to why the car won't start.
He says to look for the battery charger in the garage.
Practical mechanic Dad was, of course it's there.
I plug it in for a few hours
and it starts right up.

Packing boxes, we break for my cousin's
Homemade soup in the crockpot
I'm not taking much, the mover comes tomorrow
With the truck
Shows up right after the memorial service
Barely makes the hill as they roll in the piano
That I hope will arrive safely

My brother takes the tools, the train set
And at the last minute I pack the circular saw
So if I decide to get inspired in my own garage
And want to cut wood or make sawdust
Dad will show me how

My cousin hadn't seen my brother in 30 years
We scatter ashes in the yard
Donate bags to Goodwill and the food shelf
Find a realtor that lives down the street
My boyfriend flies home
I spend the last night I know I will ever be here
alone in their bedroom
with the sunset over the lake

On the way to the airport, the neighbor calls
Saying, "I'm the last Democrat in the neighborhood
Now that your Dad is gone." I laugh.
Dad would have liked that.

An Agnostic Ex-Catholic Will Even Sing "Ave Maria" if You Put Him in an Ozark Diner Surrounded by Enough Bible-Belters

(after a title by Marty McConnell)

—John Roche

We decide to go to Shirley's Diner,
because it's quite visible up the hill overlooking this particular Ozark divided highway,
and because my mom was named Shirley and she was a pretty good cook,
as was my future wife's mom, who was also named Shirley,
and we are burying Jules' Shirley today.

The waitress, who is not named Shirley, but maybe Ethel or Mabel or Something-Sue,
pours our table cups of slightly burned but still watery java,

Asks us which church we'd attended this morning
(it being Sunday
and none of us visibly identifiable as Jewish or Muslim or turban-clad Sikh,
though my future sister-in-law is Black and visibly uncomfortable
in this all-white diner, town, county, region).

We say we weren't at church this morning
and watch her overly mascara'd eyes grow narrow.

Then we add, "We're in town for Ma's funeral this afternoon, over at the Methodist church."

Watch her eyes spin with surprise, feigned concern, a lingering tinge of suspicion.

vii.

Moon over author's home, Albuquerque

You Can't Come Back

No, you can't come back.
You were cremated.
We scattered your ashes in the lake
Gave away your clothes
Your shoes are stacked in your garage
House up for sale
I found the lower half of your dentures
They were in the cabinet.

It's okay to visit me.
What do you miss the most?

Voice Mail

Dialing my parent's phone number
I hear Mom's voice on the line one last time
before it is disconnected
Please leave a message
Hi Mom, I learned to play a song on the piano today
Sunrise, Sunset
One of your favorites
The sheet music was in the piano bench
You and Dad were listening.

Memory House of Red in April

Red drapes shut out the blinding sun
where it's cold and dark, protect Mom's piano
a *Starck* upright, moved eight hundred miles
from Ozarks to high desert, Midwest childhood photo of me
as a toddler sitting at this same piano bench hangs in my hall
sheet music from childhood lessons
still has pencil marks and stickers of accomplishment
Mom's soprano choir voice sang Handel's Messiah,
Presbyterian and Methodist hymns, various show tunes.
Blank keys wait for me to play, my friends visit
and we try to sing the old songs, join in chorus
the piano still acclimating to low humidity
the mantel clock ticks the minutes, set on Mom's red music scarf
almost a year she's been gone.

Piano Practice

Notes transfer to my hands,
where is C, G, E without a map?
Lower clef a foreign country, a new language
semi-colon of F bass
riddled with sharps and flats, majors and minors.
Ears deceive me, need to see instead, learn to read
all over again, translating notations
to finally hear the familiar melodies
of folk songs or the great composers

One little note, grade "easy"
an adult beginner
remembers childhood practice
it seemed easier then but now I know
the stories of chords
the one stuck key.
Mom's piano in my house
her and Dad in the photo on the upright
watching, in approval.

Homesick, then

Is it the house where I grew up
a thousand miles or more away
where I rode my bike, slammed the screen door
green grass, tanning with high school friends
I barely remember? Some dead.

Parents moved away
to a place far enough to visit only once or twice a year
driving twelve hours to pull up in Dad's driveway,
he's at his workbench or out on the deck.
I tell him and Mom our old house has burned down after the sale
the new owners left a grill on, the propane tank blew up
and it all went down
nothing but ashes.
I walked the old backyard, smaller than I remember,
the tree we used to play around, summer and winter
ice or roses and tulips, now only colors.

In the Land of Lakes I lived in countless apartments,
can't remember those either except for the one with the Thai
restaurant
across the street had the best neighborhood bar
where I met lovers and friends, wrote poems on napkins
taped to the ceiling by the bartender. I hear it closed
went out of business after forty years.

After forty-eight years I left the northland for the desert
to find a new neighborhood bar where Santos hide in nichos.
I rename my fears,
escape old acquaintances, meet new ones and
one cat after another dies or comes forward.
Dust storms and red sky after a night with poets,
previous lovers find me on chat and share words never spoken
before
nothing I can do now why didn't they say those things then
new house, new love
parents die
and I scatter their ashes

in their Missouri lake
or behind New Mexico volcanoes.

Social media prompts me to wish my dead friend
a happy birthday, I already did
mailed him milagros for healing two years ago.
Mom sang in the choir, sings for me
on her recorded cd's, all I can do is cry, share it with friends
play it at her funeral.
My dead college professor still writes notes on my poems
types a letter about his life on printed letterhead from New York
sends to me overnight to meet the deadline.

They were orphans, my cousin says,
Mom and Dad, found each other
now they are ancestors
joining grandmother's lost grave in the wind.
Better see my cousin before she gets any older,
better see my parents' friends before it's too late.
Travel out of state, I left just like they did but they all come back,
anchor me through a desert ocean,
an open sea of grief.

Reconstruction of Skin

Internal
   Intermittent, organized
     structure of body
      of mind
       of internet   space and physical
     brief interval   objects   tangible gravity a dresser a
wardrobe
     left in drawers, on wire hangers, tin frames, heavy wood altar
     captured faces on skin, mirrors, paper photographs,
       legacy wanders between worlds
intermediaries, entering and exit
     lists in your handwriting, common instructions, recipes
    a ceramic jar with flowers, painted bright colors
       ground bones, ash, you picked it out for her
       where did her voice go?
       She sang in fragments, a kiss
          wool coat left over
          too small for her daughter
          happiness floats above you, whispers
             lost perfume, a scarf, pearl necklace
      rings, she worried about
          taking care of him, reconstruction
          breath
          leaving skin.

the place of bad dreams

external
   suspended, intimate
     intertwined to the place they keep naming
     like it is a place it is not
     it only seems like she is flying
        naked not: only essence with the others
        those who played her mother, grandmother, the
   great greats
        aunts, uncles, cousins, her father

fairy sprite
    flying with the plane
        in the middle of the night, she watches, knows
            how the others enter

      calls her husband, he has a double self
      that doesn't remember
                it is what it is, incoherent
                released

On the Anniversary of Dad's Death

Cries of the black cat
fill the night,
its owner missed letting him in.
All night long my old, gray cat clings
to my shoulders as we are trapped in a store
looking for food.
She doesn't know she died.
She is sweet, as always.
I rocked her in my lap a long time
before she was buried, wrapped in a towel
in a friend's backyard, underneath trees.

Will anyone more than a generation away
know where we bury our dead?
The crumbling cement stones no longer
cry out with names of importance.
Thousands, like eggs of a salmon
scattered in the river, drift downstream.
Only a few of millions will be preserved in history
for the masses to idolize.

I forgot this day until the calendar told me.
Your ashes were scattered widely,
some dumped in the lake
you loved so much.

Underworld

Little has come down to me of hers
except night visits, and Mom asks me
to replace the mattress,
make coffee, she and Dad will leave at dawn

I wear her jewelry, pearls,
the gold-emerald bracelet she gave me for a birthday
the few times out of frugality,
it sparkles at a Christmas party

I drove hundreds of miles
on New Year's Day to come home
to their house, alone and retired with the Christmas tree lit
in the corner by the window, reflecting

When they moved out of state the holiday celebrations split open
I decided to call once a week whether they called me
or not, to keep in touch, to hear about Mom falling again
they are okay, really, they say

No more sharing recipes, or the weather
news from an old neighbor,
I speak to her underwater
carry the load of the underworld
where the phones vanished
she sleeps in an unending mattress of darkness

Somewhere

This is the somewhere
We were always trying to get:
Landscape
Reduced to the basics:
Rolling mills, rocks, running
Water, burdocks, trees living and dead. (1)

Somewhere the dead
are buried under humps of dirt, somewhere
a white cross perches with faded plastic flowers run
over on the highway by drivers who will rush to get
somewhere unimportant. A basic
necessity of burial: warm landscape

soft enough to dig. We walk the land, scope
out our future with planted trees, no dead
ancestors among us. Basic
survival skills are burdock roots, some
flower stalks harvested before they get
to bloom. Tree bark stripped off as runners

to make canoes, stone faces stare at us from the bank. We run
into landscape.
Some day we will elope to a new place, get
dressed in red and tie ourselves to trees. The dead
and living surround us. Somewhere
in our pockets lie changes. BASIC

programs run on a green screen. Basic
codes run all life forms. Somewhere someone runs
deep into the forest. Ferns unfold. Some ask where
they are but we see another landscape
appear on the screen. Death
sleeps under down covers. No graveyards to get

creepy with. Graves are fine and private, we get
consolation in the land of Elysian, a basic
right of passage with manicured lawns, the dead
no longer gone but sweetly singing under running

water, weeping willows, the statuary landscape
attracting tourists with guidebooks, draped urns, winged cherubs,
somewhere

over the rainbow death got lost.
This is the somewhere we exit, back to basics.
Run to the stonecutter, chisel our own mortality.

(1) Opening stanza quote is verbatim from "Daybooks 1," Two Headed Poems, Margaret Atwood 1978.

Half

—empty, fraction
square peg in a round world

Rather be reading under the covers
all you can do
is write and listen

Refrigerator

In my parent's refrigerator
Mom kept health emergency info in a Ziploc bag
curled up between the condiments
as if a paramedic would choose to look there first.

She must have read it in a magazine.
I discovered the papers still there
while emptying the 'fridge after she died.

When Dad came to live with me
I stuffed my freezer with food he liked.
A quick meal after my work, he would be waiting.

After he died, I wondered how long I should hang onto
frozen Texas Toast and Marie Collander's meat lasagna,
items not on my grocery list, but I didn't want to go to waste.
I worked these items into my meals alone, chatting with Dad
about my day.

Two years later, the frozen strawberries
are still there in the freezer door.
Spoiled, I toss them out, make room for my life.

Laughter

We are all afraid of cliffs.
Plum blossoms float down on me over lunch
the plants, the pond.
Let go, it is okay
to rest in this moment.

Notes

Intro quote -- "In China, the lemon is the symbol of death and the lemon table is the place where men gather to talk of death" is from the book "Out of Time, the Pleasures & Perils of Ageing" by Lynne Segal p. 165

"High Bridge" – the St. Paul High Bridge is on Smith Avenue in St. Paul, Minnesota. Towering 160 feet above the Mississippi River, with spectacular views of downtown, the steel-and-concrete bridge is one of the city's most recognizable landmarks. The phrase "taking the High Bridge as a way out" has long served as a euphemism for suicide among area residents. My grandfather Milton Lindberg is buried in Union Cemetery in Maplewood, MN (a suburb of St. Paul).

"Horizons" and "I Sleep on Red Sheets" are for my maternal grandmother, Margaret Adelaide Keppler Lindberg who was murdered by my grandfather (referred to in High Bridge) due to domestic violence. She died December 26, 1939 at age 26. She is buried in Fort Madison, Iowa.

"School," "A Kind of Courage," "Roses," "What is It?" and "Somewhere" are sestinas.

"Slumber Party" – FMLA is Family Medical Leave Act

"POA" is an acronym for Power of Attorney

Manzano del Sol (apple of the sun) Good Samaratin Village is a care center in Albuquerque located at 5201 Roma Ave. NE, Albuquerque, NM 87108, where Dad passed away.

Acknowledgements

"Firstborn Brother" appeared in *Salamander* and *Appetites*

"The Other Girls Wear Dresses" appeared in *Grey Sparrow Journal*

"A Kind of Courage" appeared in *Behind the Volcanoes*

"Horizons" appeared in *Appetites*

"Lunar Elipse" appeared in *Appetites*

"Asparagus" appeared in *Appetites*

"Blind Date" appeared in *Appetites*

"Watching the Sunset with Dad on the Deck in the Ozarks Over Table Rock Lake" appeared in the *Bennington Review*

"Sunday Paper" appeared in the *Fixed & Free Anthology* & in another form in *Snow Jewel* chapbook by Grey Sparrow Press

"Lipstick" appeared in *New Mexico Elbow Room*

"Somewhere" appeared in *Behind the Volcanoes*

Other Books by Jules Nyquist

POETRY

Appetites, Beatlick Press (2012 NM/AZ Book Award finalist)

Behind the Volcanoes, Beatlick Press (2014 NM/AZ Book Award finalist)

ANTHOLOGIES (Editor)

Shadow of the Snake

Poetry in Place: Autumn Writing from the Bosque: Open Space Visitor Center

Rolling Sixes Sestinas: An Anthology of Albuquerque Poets

House of Cards: Ekphrastic Poetry: A Jules' Poetry Playhouse Project

Legends & Monsters: A Jules' Poetry Playhouse Project

Hers (Poets Speak Anthology- Volume 2)

Resources

Family Medical Leave Act (FMLA) -- enacted by President Clinton allows someone with a death of a family member (or other health issue) to take time off work, unpaid, up to 12 weeks without losing their job or health insurance. In the author's experience, after the death, FMLA does not apply. Vacation/sick time first has to be exhausted before FMLA will apply. Paperwork and reporting hours need to be filed. Check with your Human Resources Department. For more info go to: https://www.dol.gov/whd/fmla/

AARP organization – helpful with long-term care options and planning (or check with a financial advisor) www.aarp.org

Independent organizations include Meals on Wheels, Good Samaritan Society, home health care organizations, senior centers, caregivers, physical, occupational and speech therapy, social services, home safety, etc. These services are usually not covered by insurance or Medicare, although some provide services for a nominal fee. Sometimes 'gap' or supplemental insurance in addition to Medicare may cover these items.   Some assisted living or care centers do accept Medicare for a set number of days. Hospital beds and other medical equipment can be rented as needed for home use. Hospitals and Senior Centers will have helpful resources and will have numbers for 24 hour nursing help lines.

It is a good idea to have a printed list of medications to show to doctors and family members as needed. Also a list of family data and contact info.

Estate planning, advanced directives, living wills, power of attorney for health care, wills, taxes and more should be reviewed with a lawyer or other professional.

Social Security benefits are at www.ssa.gov

Probate court for those that are the executor of the estate can be found within each county. There are many on-line resources to do this yourself and forms can be downloaded. For Albuquerque, the author used http://www.bernco.gov/probate-court/default.aspx and found the staff very friendly and helpful.

Domestic violence awareness is fairly recent. The author's grandmother and others did not have the resources we do today, and domestic violence is still very much a hidden, shameful issue. Domestic violence can also run in families and can be in the form of emotional or physical abuse.

"Civil rights and anti-war movements in the 1950s and 1960s challenged the country and laid the foundation for the U.S. feminist movement. As women gained more ground in the 1970s, spousal abuse became more of a public issue. Many battered women's shelters opened in the U.S., the first being the Women's Advocates shelter in St. Paul, Minnesota in 1973.

It wasn't until 1984 that a similar bill passed through Congress, entitled The Family Violence Prevention Services Act. This act authorizes the Secretary of Health and Human Services to make grants to States to assist in supporting the establishment, maintenance, and expansion of programs and projects that prevent incidents of family violence and provide shelter and related assistance for victims and their dependents.

In the 1990s, system reforms that began in the 1980s expanded significantly and now include a focus on a broader set of systems, including welfare systems and policy issues, such as housing, mental health, substance abuse, and childcare.

Currently, there are approximately 1,900 local domestic violence programs and State domestic violence coalitions the U.S., the District of Columbia, and Puerto Rico." Source: http://www.samaritanhouseva.org/get-informed/domestic-violence/

About the Author

Jules Nyquist is the founder of Jules' Poetry Playhouse, LLC, a place for poetry and play in Albuquerque, NM. She leads creative writing classes and invites visiting poets to the Playhouse to read and share their work. She took her MFA from Bennington College, VT. She has been interviewed by New Mexico Entertainment Magazine, Minnesota Reads and other publications. Her website is www.julesnyquist.com. (Photo by John Roche)

About the Presses

Award-winning **Beatlick Press** was established in 2011 to honor the memory of Beatlick Joe Speer of Albuquerque, NM and continue his artistic mission to publish deserving writers. "Writers with something to say."
Pamela Adams Hirst, publisher. www.beatlick.com

Jules' Poetry Playhouse Publications is a division of Jules' Poetry Playhouse, LLC founded by Jules Nyquist in 2012 in Albuquerque, NM. Our publishing mission grew out of requests to record collaborations in poetry and art in book form so that we may realize our common bonds and to provide community support as readers and writers. www.julesnyquist.com

Made in the USA
Lexington, KY
11 November 2019